MAKING SENSE OF THE BIBLE

LEADER GUIDE

Also by Adam Hamilton

Adam Hamilton

Making Sense
of the Bible

Rediscovering the Power
of Scripture Today

Leader Guide
by Martha Bettis Gee

Abingdon Press
Nashville

Adam Hamilton

Making Sense of the Bible:
Rediscovering the Power of Scripture Today

Leader Guide
by Martha Bettis Gee

ISBN 978-1-4267-8558-0

14 15 16 17 18 19 20 21 22 23 — 10 9 8 7 6 5 4 3 2 1

MANUFACTURED IN THE UNITED STATES OF AMERICA

CONTENTS

To the Leader

Welcome! This is a study for those who love the Bible and look to it to help them find meaning and purpose for their lives. It is also a study for people who are willing to wrestle with portions of the Bible about which they have questions. Finally, it is a study for people who are largely unfamiliar with the Bible but who are curious and want to know more.

Adam Hamilton, author of *Making Sense of the Bible*, envisions the book as a conversation on his back porch, with each participant enjoying a glass of iced tea or lemonade. The conversation is an attempt to wrestle honestly with the tough questions often raised by thoughtful Christians and non-Christians concerning things taught in the Bible. Hamilton has sought to distill the work of scholars, while offering his own reflections as one who preaches and teaches the Bible and who regularly engages with the questions of laity and pastors alike.

The book is divided into two parts. The first section addresses some foundational questions: What is the Bible, exactly? In what sense is it God's word, and in what sense is it human reflections on God? What do we mean by calling it "inspired"? Is it inerrant or infallible as many Christians believe? This section also deals with how and when the Bible was written, the various types of writings found in it, and how and why some books made it into the Bible and some were left out.

The second section digs into troubling questions and issues, such as historical accuracy, violence, and end times. The book ends by looking at various ways to read the Bible, with the aim being for persons reading it to hear God speak through its pages and find its words to be life changing and life giving.

This six-session study makes use of the following components:

- Adam Hamilton's book *Making Sense of the Bible*;

- a DVD in which Hamilton, using stories and Scripture, presents and expands upon key points from the book;

- this Leader Guide.

Encourage participants to bring a Bible to every session. If possible, notify those interested in the study before the first session so that they can come prepared. Ask them to read the introduction and the first seven chapters in advance of the session. Then, each week, you will give participants a reading assignment for the following week. By the end of the study, they will have read the entire book.

Because of the book's length, some participants may be unable to keep up with the reading. Encourage them to come anyway because each session will include a ten- to fifteen-minute video in which Adam Hamilton presents many of the important points from the book. Our hope is that participants who don't have time to read the book during the study will turn to it afterward to explore the Bible more deeply.

Using This Guide with Your Group

Because no two groups are alike, this guide has been designed to give you as study leader some flexibility and choice in tailoring the sessions for your group. The session format is listed to assist you in your planning.

It's important to note that there are more activities in each session than most groups will have time to complete. As leader, you'll want to go over the session in advance and select the activities you think will work best for your group in the time allotted.

You may choose any or all of the activities, adapting them as you wish to meet the schedule and needs of your particular group.

The book seeks to do just as its title suggests—help to make sense of the Bible. Participants will discover a rich offering of information presented in an accessible way. Each session will cover a number of chapters and attempt to address a plethora of issues and a good deal of information. As study leader, you will want to tailor your session activities to the needs and interests of your particular group, as well as to the time frame you have available.

Session Format

Planning the Session

Session Goals
Biblical Foundation
Special Preparation

Getting Started

Opening Activity
Opening Prayer

Learning Together

Video Study and Discussion
Book Study and Discussion

Wrapping Up

Closing Activity
Closing Prayer

Helpful Hints

Preparing for the Sessions

- Pray for the leading of the Holy Spirit as you prepare for the study. Pray for discernment for yourself and for each member of the study group.

- Read the book in its entirety before the study begins. Identify which questions and issues are particularly troubling to you. Offer a special prayer that you will be open to the Spirit's movement on those issues and that you will be able to facilitate the sessions without trying to influence the group in the direction of your own leanings.

- Secure a TV and DVD player in advance.

- Before each session, familiarize yourself with the content. Read the week's book chapters again and watch the video segment.

- Choose the session elements you will use during the group session, including the specific discussion questions you plan to cover. However, be prepared to adjust the session as group members interact and as questions arise. Prepare carefully, but allow space for the Holy Spirit to move through the group members and through you as facilitator.

- Prepare the space where the session will be held so that it will enhance the learning process. Ideally, group members should be seated around a table or in a circle so that all can see each other. Because the group will often be forming pairs or small groups for discussion, movable chairs are best.

- Bring a supply of Bibles for those who forget to bring their own. Having a variety of translations is helpful.

- For most sessions you will need a chalkboard and chalk, a whiteboard and markers, or an easel with paper and markers.

Shaping the Learning Environment

- Create a climate of openness, encouraging group members to participate as they feel comfortable. Remember that some persons will jump right in with answers and comments, while others need time to process what is being discussed.

- If you notice that some group members never seem able to enter the conversation, ask if they have thoughts to share. Give everyone a chance to talk, but keep the conversation moving. Moderate to prevent a few individuals from doing all the talking.

- Communicate the importance of group discussions and group exercises.

- If no one answers at first during discussions, do not be afraid of a silence. Count silently to ten; then say something such as, "Would anyone like to go first?" If no one responds, venture an answer yourself and ask for comments.

- Model openness as you share with the group. Group members will follow your example. If you limit your sharing to a surface level, others will do the same.

- Encourage multiple answers or responses before moving on.

- To help continue a discussion and give it greater depth, ask, "Why?" or "Why do you believe that?" or "Can you say more about that?"

- Affirm others' responses with comments such as "Great," "Thanks," or "Good insight"—especially if this is the first time someone has spoken during the group session.

- Monitor your own contributions. If you are doing most of the talking, back off so that you do not train the group to listen rather than speak up.

- Remember that you do not have all the answers. Your job is to keep the discussion going and to encourage participation.

Managing the Sessions

- Begin and end on time. If a session is running longer than expected, get consensus from the group before continuing beyond the agreed-upon ending time.

- Involve group members in various aspects of the group session, such as playing the DVD, saying prayers, or reading the Scripture.

- Note that the session guides sometimes call for breaking into smaller groups or pairs. This gives everyone a chance to speak and participate fully. Mix up the groups; don't let the same people pair up for every activity.

- **One key to making sense of the Bible is the willingness to wrestle with questions and difficult issues. Participants will bring a range of understandings and opinions on these issues. The study will be most successful if group members treat one another with respect and are willing to listen to opinions that differ from their own. Work to ensure that the study offers a safe space for exploring the Bible.**

- **Because many activities call for personal sharing, confidentiality is essential. Group members should never pass along stories that have been shared in the group. Remind the group members at each session.**

SECTION ONE
THE NATURE OF SCRIPTURE

1. Making Sense of the Old Testament

Introduction; Book Chapters 1–7

Planning the Session

Session Goals

As a result of conversations and activities connected with this session, group members should begin to:

- be introduced to what the Bible is, and what it is not;

- explore the scope of Old Testament Scriptures;

- gain a basic understanding of when, how, and why Old Testament books were written;

- learn how Old Testament books came to be included in the Bible;

- get insight into how Old Testament prophecy is reinterpreted through the lens of the life of Jesus Christ.

Biblical Foundation

The devil said to [Jesus], "If you are the Son of God, command this stone to become a loaf of bread." Jesus answered him, "It is written, 'One does not live by bread alone.'"

Luke 4:3-4

Special Preparation

- Adam Hamilton envisions this study as a conversation on his back porch with refreshments. If you like, plan to bring iced tea and lemonade along with cups or glasses and napkins.

- Write the following question on a large sheet of paper: What is one thing about the Bible that has troubled, perplexed, or confused you? Why?

- Prepare two additional sets of large paper sheets. In the first set, prepare five sheets, each with one of the following headings: Owner's Manual, Magic 8 Ball, Book of Systematic Theology, Science Textbook, and Book of Promises. In the second set, prepare four sheets, each with one of the following headings: The Law, Historical Books, Poetical and Wisdom Books, and The Prophets.

- Print the children's song "The B-I-B-L-E" and post it. (Words are shown later in this chapter under Learning Together.)

- Although not essential, a wall map of the Ancient Near East in Old Testament times would be helpful. You'll also find maps in the book chapter.

- **Remember that there are more activities than most groups will have time to complete. As leader, you'll want to go over the session in advance and select the activities you think will work best for your group in the time allotted.**

GETTING STARTED

Opening Activity

In a prominent location, post the question you wrote on a large sheet of paper in your preparation. As group members arrive, welcome them to the study. If members are not familiar with one another, provide nametags. Supply Bibles for those who did not bring one.

Gather together, and have group members introduce themselves. Ask them to name a favorite book of the

Bible or to tell a Scripture they remember. Call attention to the question you posted on the large sheet of paper:

- What is one thing about the Bible that has troubled, perplexed, or confused you? Why?

Form pairs and invite participants to take time to discuss this question. Then reassemble as a large group and ask participants to name the issues and questions that surfaced in their one-on-one discussions. List these on a large sheet of paper.

Ask the group to read over quickly the Introduction to Adam Hamilton's book *Making Sense of the Bible*. Point out that Hamilton envisions the book as a conversation with his readers, sitting on the back porch and sharing glasses of iced tea or lemonade. If you have chosen to provide these refreshments, invite participants to help themselves to some.

Ask group members to turn to the book's table of contents. Point out that the book is divided into two parts. The first part, "The Nature of Scripture," addresses some foundational questions, such as how the Bible was written and in what sense it is inspired, as well as what types of writing are included and the criteria used to decide which books were to be included. In the second part, "Making Sense of the Bible's Challenging Passages," some difficult questions and issues will be addressed, such as science and religion, historical accuracy, and end times. Look again at the large sheet of paper with questions contributed by participants, and note which of their questions will be addressed in the book.

Invite a volunteer to read aloud one of the final paragraphs of Hamilton's Introduction, beginning with the words "I hear God speak through the Bible." Encourage participants to bring an open mind and heart to this study. During this study, they will wrestle with thorny passages while at the same time listening for the One to whom the entire Bible bears witness.

Opening Prayer

Open our ears, O God, to what you would have us hear. Through your holy Word, convict us, challenge us, and comfort us. Open our minds to new insights and fresh perspectives about our questions. Open our hearts to the moving of your Spirit. In the name of Jesus Christ your Son. Amen.

LEARNING TOGETHER

Video Study and Discussion

Briefly introduce Adam Hamilton, the book author and video presenter. From his website at www. adamhamilton.org, visitors learn that Adam Hamilton is senior pastor of The United Methodist Church of the Resurrection in Leawood, Kansas, where he preaches to more than 8,000 per week. Hamilton states that he writes and teaches on life's tough questions, the doubts with which we all wrestle, and the challenging issues we face today. He explores the "gray" areas that present themselves when the Bible's teachings cross paths with our life experiences. Participants can learn more about Hamilton and his books at www.adamhamilton.org.

Call attention to the large sheet of paper with the children's song, "The B-I-B-L-E." If possible, sing it together:

The B-I-B-L-E!
Yes, that's the book for me!
I stand alone on the Word of God,
The B-I-B-L-E!

The B-I-B-L-E,
Yes, that's the book for me,
I read and pray, trust and obey,
The B-I-B-L-E.

Invite the group to think about what this song says about the nature of the Bible.

- What does it mean to "stand alone on the Word of God"?

- What does it mean to "trust and obey" the Bible? Does this meaning imply that we must accept that every word of the Bible has an equal claim on us?

- Does this childhood song reflect the way you view the Bible? If so, in what ways? If not, why?

Play the video. Before starting, set the stage by inviting group members to listen for Adam Hamilton's story of his own encounter with what he calls the "words of life." After viewing the video, discuss the following:

- In your understanding of the Bible, how do you balance the concepts of divinity and humanity?

- Hamilton observes that he struggles with the biblical text; yet, even in the face of his disagreement with some Scripture passages, God speaks to him through the text. What is your experience of wrestling with biblical texts?

Invite any other observations participants may want to share about this video segment. Explain that in upcoming session videos, the group will explore information about how we got the Bible and how and by whom it was written, using the information from Hamilton's book.

Book Study and Discussion

Form five groups. Give each group one of the five large sheets of paper you prepared in the first set of sheets: Owner's Manual, Magic 8 Ball, Book of Sysematic Theology, Science Textbook, Book of Promises. (See Special Preparation, earlier in this chapter.) Ask each group to scan the information in Chapter 1, paying special attention to the information about the heading on their sheet. Then ask them to discuss that particular way of characterizing the Bible and to write their thoughts on the large sheet of paper.

Reconvene the large group and ask each small group to share its thoughts and comments. Discuss:

- Is there one of these characterizations that in some way appeals to you? If so, why?

- What are the inadequacies Hamilton reveals in each of these ways of characterizing the Bible?

- How might the assumptions behind each approach to reading the Bible leave readers confused, misguided, or disappointed?

Explore the Timeline and Map

In preparation for Chapter 3's fifteen-minute tour of the Old Testament, list on a large sheet of paper the dates shown in the text that represent the current consensus view of science regarding the origin of the universe. Then ask participants to scan the Chapter 2 timeline quickly for events described in the Bible up to the point when the Old Testament period ends (400s B.C.). Invite them to name any observations that seem particularly relevant to them (for example, the striking difference between the scientific consensus for the earth's creation and the traditional dating on the timeline). Also have them examine the maps included in the chapter, making note of the area of the Fertile Crescent. If you have a wall map showing the Ancient

Near East, ask volunteers to point out the relevant locations. Ask:

- What was the strategic significance of the area we call the Holy Land?

Emphasize that because of its location and its significance as a major land trade route, this part of the world has been coveted by major powers for millennia.

The Old Testament in Fifteen Minutes

Invite the group to spend fifteen minutes "walking" through the Old Testament as suggested by Adam Hamilton in order to review the scope of the Old Testament.

Form four groups. Give each group one of the four large sheets of paper you prepared in the second set of sheets: The Law, Historical Books, Poetical and Wisdom Books, and The Prophets. (See Special Preparation, earlier in this chaper.) Ask each group to read the text in Chapter 3 relevant to their category of the Old Testament and work together to print a brief summary, including the names of the books, on the sheet. Allow ten minutes or so for groups to work, then ask them to share their information with the large group.

The Writing of the Old Testament

Recall Hamilton's story from the video about his airplane conversation on the subject of the Bible. Invite participants to read the first paragraphs of Chapter 4 silently. Tell the group that this chapter addresses questions of how the Old Testament was written, if not literally inscribed by the finger of God on stone tablets.

As a large group, look at the sheets of paper completed by each of the small groups. Underline the names of the first five books of the Bible and label them as Torah. Ask the group to scan the second paragraph of Chapter 4 and give other names for those five books (the Pentateuch, the Law of God, the Books of the Covenant, the Law of Moses, the Books of Moses, and Moses). Jot down these names on the sheet.

Explore the question of whether or not Moses wrote these five books. Ask volunteers to read aloud the following verses: Genesis 12:6, Numbers 12:3, Deuteronomy 34:1-12, Deuteronomy 31:24, and Exodus 24:4. Discuss:

- What hints do these verses give us about the assertion that Moses himself wrote the Torah in its entirety?

- What do these verses indicate about the writing of the portion of the Bible identified as the Law?

- What does Adam Hamilton suggest as a reasonable hypothesis about the authorship of these books?

Hamilton observes that the Exodus event and the giving of the Law are Israel's defining story. To set the stage for discussing what he identifies as another event influencing the shaping of the Old Testament, print "911" on a large sheet of paper or a board. Invite participants to name the first thing that comes to mind. Prior to September 11, 2001, most people would probably have named the number we call in an emergency. However, since that date, the attacks on the World Trade Center and the Pentagon likely come to mind first. Form pairs and ask participants to discuss the following question with their partners.

- Where were you on September 11, 2001? What do you remember?

In the large group, discuss participants' memories. How many people remember exactly what they were doing, how they felt when they heard or saw the news, what they were wearing, or what the weather was like?

Ask a volunteer to read aloud 2 Kings 25:1-21. Then invite the group to close their eyes as you read aloud the paragraph in Chapter 4 of the book beginning "It was the summer of 587 B.C."

Adam Hamilton notes the impact of the Temple's destruction on the Jews and invites us to imagine that on 9/11 the entire city of Washington was destroyed, the president was blinded and led away in chains, his family killed, and then the entire nation was overrun with foreign troops. Request participants to keep their eyes closed and imagine such a scenario. Ask:

- How has 9/11 shaped our nation's subsequent history in the past decade?

- If the more catastrophic scenario described above had in fact come to pass, how might that event have changed our lives?

Hamilton observes:

> It was during this time [the two decades before the Exile and the subsequent fifty years of exile], many biblical scholars believe, that most of the Old Testament took its final form as the Jews reflected upon their story, sought to make sense of their plight, and focused on once more being God's covenant people.

To get a sense of the Babylonian Exile's influence on the Torah, ask volunteers to read aloud Deuteronomy 31:14-29.

The Old Testament Canon

Explain that the word *canon* means rule or standard and that canonization is the process by which certain writings came to be included in the Bible. Invite someone to tell how many books are in the Old Testament (we would say 39). Hamilton points out that the number of books in the Old Testament—the Hebrew Scriptures—

depends on whom you ask. Jews, Catholics, Orthodox Christians, and Protestants would each give a different answer.

If they have not already done so, allow a few minutes for group participants to read over the information in Chapter 5, then discuss:

- What are some differences in how Jews and Christians categorize the books of Hebrew Scripture and in how they order them?

- Adam Hamilton notes that history is told from the perspective of the teller in order to meet the needs of people in a given time. For example, what differences does he note in how Samuel and Chronicles tell the story of David?

- Which books would a rabbi call the most authoritative? Which books would you name?

- Hamilton notes that for Jews, books of the Torah convey, in a special way, God's will and purposes for God's people. How do you respond?

Hamilton observes that the process by which the Old Testament documents came to be canonized was a bit messy and that the question of what belongs in the Old Testament is still being debated by some Christians. Invite participants to give an example or two of how the process evolved.

Jesus and the Old Testament

Book Chapter 6 invites us to consider what Scriptures were significant to Jesus. Ask a volunteer to read aloud Luke 2:42-50. Adam Hamilton notes in Chapter 6 that a boy began studying the Scriptures at age five and the Mishnah (the Jewish oral tradition) at age ten so that at age thirteen he could become an adult. Today this is codified as the Bar Mitzvah. Hamilton observes that the three books to which Jesus alludes most often were Psalms, Isaiah, and Deuteronomy, one from each category of the Tanakh.

Form three groups and assign one of the following Scriptures or pairs of Scriptures to each group: Deuteronomy 6 and Luke 4:1-13; Ezekiel 34; and Isaiah 53 and Zechariah 9:9. Ask each group to read the Scripture and the relevant text in book Chapter 6. In the large group, discuss:

- In what ways would you say your assigned passage may have shaped Jesus' understanding of his life and mission?

- Adam Hamilton observes that Jesus' ethic was a call to live in radical obedience to God— both a call to holiness of heart and life and an emphasis on God's grace and concern for sinners. How would you say Jesus both embodied what the Hebrew Scriptures exemplified and imbued them with new meaning?

- How did Jesus himself summarize the Scriptures? (See Matthew 22:37-40.)

Prophecy, the Old Testament, and the Early Church

Invite participants to take turns reading aloud Luke 24:13-34. Adam Hamilton observes that it was in both the breaking of the bread and the hearing of Scripture that the disciples on the Emmaus road encountered the risen Christ. Hamilton reminds us that the Scriptures Jesus was interpreting were Hebrew Scriptures of Moses and the prophets. The early church, in reading those Scriptures, saw them through the lens of the resurrected Christ. To see an example of how Old Testament prophecies were fulfilled in the New Testament, invite someone to read aloud Matthew 1:18-25.

Have someone else read aloud the paragraph in book Chapter 7 beginning, "But grab your Bible and open it to Isaiah 7 and look at the context," and then have someone read Isaiah 7:14. Ask the group to read silently Hamilton's subsequent paragraphs, which give information about the passage. Ask:

- Within the context in which Isaiah was written, who do you think is the young woman to whom the passage refers? Is it Mary the mother of Jesus or someone else?

Invite the group to read Isaiah 7:10-17 and apply the three questions Hamilton suggests:

1. What did these words mean when Isaiah first wrote them? How were they understood by the people he was addressing?

2. How did Jesus and the early church reapply and reinterpret these words? What did they mean to Jesus as he was preparing for the cross? What did they mean to the early Christians as they reflected on the life, death, and resurrection of Jesus?

3. What might the words mean for my life today? What would God want me to hear from them now?

Discuss the following:

* Hamilton writes that it may be helpful to know that the Greek word translated as "fulfill" can also mean "complete." In light of that information, how would you explain how these prophecies function?

WRAPPING UP

Closing Activity

Ask participants to sum up this first session by responding to the following open-ended prompts:

- In learning more about the Hebrew Scriptures,
  I was struck by ...
  I still have some confusion or questions about ...
  I want to think further about ...

Encourage the group to read book Chapters 8–13 prior to the next session.

Closing Prayer

We thank you, O Holy One, for the wonderful words of life. Guide us in the coming days as we continue to explore what your Word meant—to the ancient community to which it was addressed, to Jesus, and to the early church. Most of all, by your Spirit, guide us as together we seek to discern what your Word means for us today and what you would have us to hear today. In the name of your son Jesus Christ. Amen.

2. Making Sense of the New Testament

Book Chapters 8–13

Planning the Session

Session Goals

As a result of conversations and activities connected with this session, group members should begin to:

- examine which Hebrew Scriptures were significant to Jesus;

- explore the scope of New Testament Scriptures;

- gain a basic understanding of when, how, and why New Testament books were written;

- be introduced to how New Testament books came to be included in the Bible.

Biblical Foundation

"'You shall love the Lord your God with all
your heart, and with all your soul, and with all
your mind.' This is the greatest and first com-
mandment. And a second is like it: 'You shall love
your neighbor as yourself.' On these two commandments hang all the law and the prophets."

Matthew 22:37b-40

Special Preparation

- If you served iced tea and lemonade in the last
  session, continue to do so. Bring iced tea and
  lemonade, along with cups or glasses and
  napkins.

- Prepare a large sheet of paper with the headings
  "The Synoptic Gospels" and "John."

- Although not essential, a wall map of the
  Ancient Near East in New Testament times
  would be helpful.

- **Remember that there are more activities
  than most groups will have time to complete.
  As leader, you'll want to go over the session
  in advance and select the activities you
  think will work best for your group in the
  time allotted.**

GETTING STARTED

Opening Activity

As group members arrive, welcome them. Be sure each participant has a Bible, and provide Bibles for those who did not bring one.

Gather together. Using the large sheets of paper from the previous session, review what the Bible is and is not, as well as the basic divisions of Old Testament books. Invite those who were in attendance to name one insight they gained in exploring the Old Testament and how it came to be. Remind participants that, as they encounter the Scripture together and wrestle with questions they have, they can be sure of the presence of the Holy Spirit.

Opening Prayer

Come, Holy Spirit. We yearn to encounter you, the Living God, as we explore the New Testament Scriptures. Be present today, and guide us to deeper understandings of your Holy Word. Amen.

LEARNING TOGETHER

Video Study and Discussion

Ask the group to indicate, with a show of hands, if they have read Dan Brown's novel *The Da Vinci Code* or seen the movie based on the book. Invite anyone who has done so to tell what the story includes that runs counter to the New Testament (for example, that Mary Magdalene and Jesus were married, or that she was of the tribe of Benjamin). Invite the group to look for what Adam Hamilton has to say in the video about Dan Brown's story and the reliability of the New Testament.

Show the video, and then discuss the following:

- Hamilton observes that Jesus never wrote anything. What does Hamilton mean when he says that Jesus is not only the messenger, he is the message?

- What is *kerygma*? What is its significance? How did the oral tradition shape what became the Gospels?

- How does the Gospel of John differ from the other three Gospels?

Encourage the group to keep in mind what the video communicates about how the New Testament was shaped and the criteria used to determine which books became a part of it. That information will inform the more in-depth exploration during the rest of the session.

Book Study and Discussion
The New Testament in Fifteen Minutes

As Adam Hamilton suggests, ask participants to put a finger at the end of Malachi, where the Old Testament ends, and another at the last chapter of Revelation, the end of the New Testament. Hamilton tells us that there are approximately 23,145 verses in the Protestant Old Testament and 7,958 in the New Testament, so the Old Testament comprises 75 percent of our Bible and the New Testament 25 percent.

On a large sheet of paper, list the categories of Old Testament books discussed in the previous session: The Law, Historical Books, Poetical and Wisdom Books, and The Prophets. Ask the group to scan the text in Chapter 8 and to name the books in the New Testament that roughly correspond with any of the categories in the Old Testament. List these books on the other side of the large sheet of paper.

Form two groups. Ask one group to read the information in the text about the Gospels and to record any relevant information on a large sheet of paper. Also encourage them to recall additional information they remember from the video segment. Ask the other group to do the same for the Letters. In the large group, ask both small groups to share their information. Invite participants to add other relevant details that come to mind on each of the two sheets. Finally, give consideration to the book of Revelation. Ask participants to suggest facts to add to a third sheet about Revelation.

Before moving on to consider the New Testament books in more depth, remind the group what Adam

Hamilton has to say about the power of the New Testament message to change lives. What was his own story of being transformed by reading it?

Ask the group to remember that although they are gaining new knowledge about the Bible, it is not for the purpose of information but transformation.

Reading Someone Else's Letters

On the timeline in Chapter 2, ask group members to locate the chronology of the New Testament and to refer to it as they review the information about Paul in book Chapter 9. Invite participants to name relevant dates for the New Testament, beginning with the date of Jesus' birth (4 B.C.).

Ask a volunteer to read aloud Acts 8:1-3. What picture of Saul is painted here? Then have participants read silently Acts 9:1-19. Discuss:

- Recall what Hamilton says about Jesus in the video segment: that Jesus is not only the messenger but also the message. How do you see this reflected in Paul's conversion?

- How was Paul transformed by his encounter with Jesus?

- What does Hamilton mean when he says that in reading the Epistles, we are reading someone else's mail? How does it make a difference to keep this in mind?

If you have a wall map, or if you use the map in Hamilton's book, ask a volunteer to locate Cyprus and Turkey. If the map is one of the Near East in New Testament times, have someone point out Galatia.

Form small groups of three or four participants. Ask the groups to review what Hamilton writes in Chapter 9 about Paul's letter to the Galatians and to read some of the Galatians passages from the Bible. When groups have had a few minutes to work, ask each group to report two or three points Hamilton makes that seem important in understanding the letter. List the points on a large sheet of paper, then discuss:

- Hamilton observes that the two poles of legalism and libertinism, if carried to extremes, were in the time of the Galatians capable of wrecking the Christian faith. In what ways are these extremes still a problem?

- How does the letter to the Galatians help us in navigating between these two poles?

- Hamilton also notes that Galatians and the other letters addressed specific first-century cultural practices in a very different world. He suggests that there is room to ask questions of how to apply the letters to our own lives. Would you agree? Why or why not?

Questions of Authorship

Ask participants to scan Chapter 10, which addresses the question of who wrote Paul's letters. Note that scholars believe Paul dictated some letters to an amanuensis, or scribe. Ask:

- Which letters are the Deutero-Pauline or "disputed" letters?

- What are some of the reasons these letters are questioned?

Invite the group members to respond to the following statement:

- The biblical documents were written and edited by people who were addressing the needs of the people of their time. These same documents, as complicated as their composition and final editing may have been, are also said to be inspired by God, and in and through them God continues to speak to us today.

The Gospels

Have the group return to the timeline in Chapter 2. Note that most biblical scholars believe the Gospels were written between A.D. 70 and 85. Ask:

- What does Hamilton suggest was the precipitating factor in their writing? (Note that earlier accounts were written in the A.D. 50s and 60s while the apostles were still alive.)

- What is the Synoptic Problem?

Tell the group that first they will look at the three Synoptic Gospels: Matthew, Mark, and Luke. Form three small groups and assign one of the three Synoptic Gospels to each group. Ask them to read the material in Chapter 11 related to their assigned Gospel. Suggest that each group pay particular attention to the diagrams in the chapter. On a large sheet of paper, ask them to record significant information about their Gospel, including the sources each Gospel writer used, the approximate date, the community to which the Gospel might have been addressed, and what the text has to say about themes. As a large group, look at the three sheets and discuss:

- What is the relationship among the Gospels of Matthew, Mark, and Luke?

- Does the Four-Source (or Two-Source) Hypothesis seem credible to you? Does this theory diminish in any way your understanding of the Gospels as Good News? Why or why not?

- Based on this information, what would you say about the reliability of the Gospel accounts?

Note that 92 percent of John's Gospel is not in the Synoptics. Ask participants to scan Chapter 12. Point

out the large sheet of paper with the Gospel headings. Ask the group to name differences between
the Gospels of Matthew, Mark, and Luke on one hand,
and the Gospel of John on the other. Jot down these
differences on the sheet under the appropriate heading.
Based on what the small groups have charted, invite the
large group to make observations about the differences.
Discuss:

- Hamilton offers a possible explanation for the
  divide between mainline and conservative
  churches. What is it? Would you agree?

Which Books Were Included?

Remind participants of Hamilton's observation in
the video segment: Jesus was not only the messenger but the message. Ask a volunteer to read aloud
Acts 2:22-24. Note that Hamilton says the primary
"text" for the apostles' preaching was the death and
resurrection of Jesus Christ.

Ask a volunteer to read 2 Peter 3:15-16. What four
things does Hamilton want us to note in this passage?
(See Chapter 13.)

If participants have not already done so, ask them
to read silently the material about the emergence of the
Gospels as Scripture. Note that by the end of the first
century, there was not yet a formal New Testament in
circulation. Ask the group to refer to the information
about the second, third, and fourth centuries, and name

what they consider significant people or events in the formation of the New Testament.

Look together at the four criteria Hamilton cites for inclusion of books in the canon. Invite volunteers to define and summarize briefly the four criteria. Ask:

- What does Hamilton have to say about a fifth suggested criterion, inspiration?

- Hamilton notes that the process by which the church ultimately settled on inclusion does not read like a mystery novel filled with conspiracies and intrigue. Based on the criteria and the process, would you agree? Why or why not?

- Hamilton observes that the story of the New Testament's canonization allows him to see the New Testament's humanity, a product of human authors inspired by God who wrote to meet the needs of their time. What does this say to you about how God spoke and continues to speak through Scripture?

WRAPPING UP

Closing Activity

Ask participants to sum up the second session by responding to the following open-ended prompts:

- In learning more about the New Testament,
  I was struck by …
  I still have some confusion or questions about …
  I want to think further about …

Emphasize that this session, like the previous one, has covered a staggering amount of information. If participants have not yet had time to read the first thirteen chapters, encourage them to do so. Also encourage them to reflect on the following questions as they read Scripture during their time of devotion in the coming week:

- What is the context of the words I am reading? What was the writer trying to say to the people?

- What is my context? How is God speaking to me through these words?

Tell the group that in the next session they will be considering whether the Bible is the inspired Word of God, how God speaks through the Bible, and the troubling question of whether the Bible is ever wrong. Encourage participants to read book Chapters 14–18.

Closing Prayer

Gracious God, we give thanks for your son Jesus Christ, who was not only the messenger, he was the message. We give thanks for those first-century authors who demonstrate the New Testament's humanity. Open our hearts that we might continue to be transformed by your living word. In the name of Jesus, the message. Amen.

3. Questions about the Nature of Scripture

Book Chapters 14–18

Planning the Session

Session Goals

As a result of conversations and activities connected with this session, group members should begin to:

- examine understandings of how the Bible was inspired;

- explore ways in which the Bible is the Word of God and how God may be speaking in and through people;

- wrestle with the question of whether the Bible is inerrant and infallible;

- consider how to evaluate whether a passage continues to reflect God's will for God's people;

- celebrate Scripture as a living, breathing document.

Biblical Foundation

Jacob was left alone; and a man wrestled with him until daybreak. …But Jacob said, "I will not let you go, unless you bless me."

Genesis 32:24; 26*b*

Special Preparation

- If you are providing iced tea and lemonade, continue to provide it along with cups or glasses and napkins.

- On a whiteboard or large sheet of paper, print the following passage that Hamilton quotes in Chapter 14: "Inspiration awakens us to new possibilities by allowing us to transcend our ordinary experiences and limitations. Inspiration propels a person from apathy to possibility, and transforms the way we perceive our own capabilities."[1]

[1] Scott Barry Kaufman, "Why Inspiration Matters," *HBR Blog Network*, November 8, 2011, http://blogs.hbr.org/cs/2011/11/why_inspiration_matters.html.

- On another sheet, print the following:

  1. Authors write Scriptures.
  2. God breathes on them.
  3. The words come to life.

- On a different sheet, make a chart listing Matthew 28, Mark 16, Luke 24, and John 20–22 vertically down the sheet. Across the top, list the following: Who went to the tomb? How many angels? Who rolled away the stone? What happened after the Resurrection?

- **Remember that there are more activities than most groups will have time to complete. As leader, you'll want to go over the session in advance and select the activities you think will work best for your group in the time allotted.**

GETTING STARTED

Opening Activity

As group members arrive, welcome them. Be sure each participant has a Bible and provide Bibles for those who did not bring one.

Gather together. Ask volunteers to name an insight from last session's discussion about how the New Testament came to be. Review Adam Hamilton's assertion that

Jesus was not just the messenger but also the message. In this session, the group will begin to explore the nature of Scripture—in what ways we can say it was inspired by God and is God's Word, how God speaks in and through it, and whether the claim can be made that Scripture is infallible and inerrant.

Opening Prayer

Holy God, we long to hear your Word for us today. We yearn to have a better understanding of the Bible. By your Spirit, make us receptive to what will be revealed as we wrestle with Scripture. Amen.

LEARNING TOGETHER

Video Study and Discussion

Explain that in this video segment, Adam Hamilton reiterates what he feels to be some misunderstandings of the Bible and how it functions. Invite the group to listen when Hamilton describes the way the Bible works as both the Word of God and the words of the people.

After viewing the segment, discuss:

- What are some ways Hamilton says God speaks to us? How have you experienced the Word of God coming to you?

- What does Hamilton mean when he says that, in a sense, Scripture is a sacrament?

- How does the word of God become the Word of God for us? What is necessary for us to do?

- Describe what Hamilton means when he says Jesus Christ is the unmitigated Word of God.

- How do the great commandments (love God and neighbor) function as a colander?

Invite a volunteer to read aloud the account of Jacob wrestling with God in Genesis 32:22-32. In a similar way, Hamilton is giving us permission—strongly encouraging us—to wrestle with Scripture. Invite participants to recall some of the questions they posed as troubling at the beginning of Session 1. How might these questions be used to wrestle with Scripture?

Book Study and Discussion
The Inspiration of Scripture

Call the group's attention to the quotation you posted from Chapter 14 ("Inspiration awakens us to new possibilities ..."). Invite them to consider the examples Hamilton includes of persons who responded to the power of Scripture and who were moved to take transformative action. Invite participants to describe similar experiences they may have had in which they were inspired by Scripture or in which Scripture illumined them. Ask:

- When and how are you most likely to hear God speaking to you through the words of Scripture?

Beyond the question of how Scripture inspires us, Hamilton invites us to consider how God inspired the human beings who recorded Scripture. Invite a volunteer to read aloud 2 Timothy 3:16-17, the only place in all of the Bible where we find the phrase "inspired by God."

- According to Hamilton, to what Scriptures was Paul referring when he used the phrase "all Scripture"?

Note that the Greek word for the phrase "inspired by God" was apparently created by Paul and is used nowhere else in the Bible or in the Greek language until after Paul's time.

Call the group's attention to the posted phrases from Chapter 14 that describe what Paul may have meant by the phrase "God breathed." Ask participants to scan the text where Hamilton uses other Scriptures to further our understanding of what the early church meant by the term *inspiration* (beginning with "There are other scriptures …").

- Hamilton suggests the apostles believed that the sacred writings were influenced in some way by the Holy Spirit and that the writings spoke not only to the people of that time but also pointed ahead in some way to the time of Christ. How do you respond?

- What is your response to Hamilton's question about whether the guidance a pastor seeks from the Holy Spirit before preaching is the same as that received by the writers of Scripture? Does the inspiration of the New Testament writings differ, and if so, in what ways?

Debate Verbal, Plenary Inspiration

Arbitrarily form two groups to debate the affirmative and negative of the proposition below. (Note that some participants may need to debate positions different from the positions they hold.)

Resolved: The Bible is literally the Word of God, virtually dictated by God.

Allow a few minutes for each group to prepare its case using information from the book and from their own experiences. Choose one or two persons to debate. Then hold the debate. Allow each side two minutes to present its case and one minute for rebuttal. Those participants not debating can serve as the audience.

Following the debate, debrief the experience. Which arguments were the most persuasive to the group? Why? For those debating a position different from their own, how did it feel? What did they learn?

The Word of God?

Invite a volunteer to read aloud John 1:1, 14. Discuss:

- What does Adam Hamilton mean when he says Jesus is the definitive, unmitigated Word of God?

- Hamilton asserts that some of what we read in the Bible is clearly not God's Word to us. What are some examples he cites? If you agree, what are some examples you would identify from your own reading of Scripture? If you disagree, what are some reasons you would cite?

As Hamilton suggests, ask the group to consider some of the forty-one passages in the Bible where the phrase "the word of God" is used. (He also notes another 260 passages that refer to "the word of the Lord.") Assign the following verses to pairs or small groups:

- Luke 3:2-3

- Luke 5

- Luke 8

- Acts 4:31

- 1 Peter 1:23-25

Ask the group to read each passage and try to discern what it is saying about the word of God, and then read the portion of book Chapter 15 that refers to those verses. Discuss:

- Hamilton observes that the phrase "the word of God" is almost always a message from God—an attempt to reveal God's purposes, character, and will. Do the verses you read back this up?

- Hamilton observes that the Bible is not an autobiography; it is a biography. What does he mean, and how do you respond to his statement?

Inerrancy and Infallibility

Ask someone to read aloud the paragraph from the Chicago Statement on Biblical Inerrancy that is cited by Hamilton in Chapter 17. Have another volunteer read the definition of inerrancy offered by Dr. Paul Feinberg, one of the authors of the Chicago statement who was attempting to explain the group's position. (In Hamilton's book, Feinberg's definition is shown just below the Chicago statement.) Ask:

- What two reasons does Adam Hamilton give for not adopting the view of the Chicago group?

- What are some reasons supporters of inerrancy give to account for inconsistencies and apparent errors found in Scripture?

One of the foundational stories Hamilton invites us to consider in the biblical narrative is the Resurrection. Invite the group to form four small groups. Have each small group read over one of the Gospel accounts of the Resurrection (Matthew 28, Mark 16, Luke 24, and John 20–22) as well as the material in Hamilton's book discussing each account. Reconvene the large group, and on the chart you prepared before the session, record the details of each account in the columns provided: Who went to the tomb? How many angels? Who rolled away the stone? What happened after the Resuurection? Discuss:

- Where are the four accounts in agreement? Where do they differ?

- How would you account for the differences? Do they make a difference to your faith?

- Hamilton notes that the supporters of inerrancy ask two questions. What are the questions, and how does he respond? Are you in agreement with his answers, or would you have a different response?

Distribute paper and pens or pencils. Invite participants to consider the doctrine of Scripture held by the supporters of verbal, plenary inspiration and biblical inerrancy. Then ask them to read over the statement of the Church of England that was adopted later by John Wesley. Ask participants to formulate their own brief doctrine of Scripture. Allow a few minutes for work, and then encourage them to continue to reflect on and to refine their doctrines in the coming week.

Views of Scripture

Hamilton proposes an alternative to the claim made by supporters of verbal, plenary inspiration and inerrancy that their view of Scripture is "high." Ask someone to summarize briefly the view of those supporters, as stated at the beginning of Chapter 18.

Then ask a volunteer to read the next-to-last paragraph of the chapter, in which Hamilton states his own view. Discuss:

- Hamilton believes there are some Scriptures that no longer fully reflect God's heart, character, or will, and perhaps never did. How does he respond to the valid question of how we can know which Scriptures are binding upon us and which Scriptures we can set aside? How would you answer that question?

- Hamilton observes that liberals and conservatives alike pick and choose what they will emphasize to support their own particular biases. Can you think of examples from both sides?

- What is Hamilton's proposal for how we examine and interpret all Scripture? What lens does he suggest we use? What other tools are available to help us make sense of difficult passages?

WRAPPING UP

Closing Activity

Invite the group members to look up Acts 15:1-21 and read the passage aloud. Hamilton observes about this passage:

What happened was the recognition that parts of the Bible no longer reflected God's will for his people. This determination was made based on a theme of the Old Testament (that God would draw the Gentiles to himself), theological reflection upon the nature of the new covenant Jesus had instituted, conversation among the disciples, and the observation that the Holy Spirit had already been poured out upon the Gentiles even without circumcision.

Tell participants that in the next three sessions they will consider difficult questions and issues that emerge from Scripture. During those sessions you will be referring to how the disciples came to consensus and perhaps drawing on and making use of their criteria.

During the coming week, encourage group members to continue reflecting on and adding to their own statement of how to view Scripture. Also, ask that they read Chapters 19–21 in preparation for the session and that they review the information from earlier chapters and sessions.

Closing Prayer

Gracious God, guide us as we explore our questions about Scripture. Speak to us in and through the Bible. Give us ears to hear and minds and hearts to discern your will. Amen.

SECTION TWO
MAKING SENSE OF THE BIBLE'S
CHALLENGING PASSAGES

4. The Bible and Science

Book Chapters 19–21

Planning the Session

Session Goals

As a result of conversations and activities connected with this session, group members should begin to:

- wrestle with some questions about Scripture and science, using the previous session's background as a foundation;

- explore the kind of truths the archetypal stories in Genesis are communicating;

- contrast those truths with scientific truths about the origins of the earth, and examine whether the two types of truths are in conflict;

- be introduced to one ancient flood account, the Gilgamesh Epic;

- experience the difference between a historic and scientific account of creation, compared with a poetic and archetypal account, and be able to express what each communicates.

Biblical Foundation

These things happened to them to serve as an example, and they were written down to instruct us, on whom the ends of the ages have come.

1 Corinthians 10:11

Special Preparation

- If you have been providing iced tea and lemonade, continue to do so.

- Should you choose to show the YouTube video or Internet image described below, be sure to arrange for a laptop and projector.

- If you would like to show a YouTube video of James Weldon Johnson's *God's Trombones* as described in the session plan, preview and choose a segment from those avaiable. One version is https://www.youtube.com/watch?feature=player_detailpage&v=Kl9smMM07N8. Arrange to download the video to a laptop and to get a video projector.

- If possible, do an Internet search for an image of *The Creation of Adam* by Michelangelo, the image on the ceiling of the Sistine Chapel. One source is at https://www.google.com/#q=sistine+chapel+ceiling+creation+of+adam+michelangelo. Download the image to a laptop for projection.

- Gather art and writing materials (paper, pens, colored markers, crayons, and the like). On a large sheet of paper, post the following three questions from Chapter 21:

  1. Was there a Noah? Did floodwaters really cover the whole earth and destroy every living thing except what was on the ark?

  2. How do we reckon with the morality of God sending such universal destruction such that every terrestrial creature, including every human being, was destroyed?

  3. What do we make of the connection between the story of Noah and flood stories that appear in other ancient cultures?

- **Remember that there are more activities than most groups will have time to complete. As leader, you'll want to go over the session in advance and select the activities you think will work best for your group in the time allotted.**

GETTING STARTED

Opening Activity

Welcome participants as they arrive. Provide Bibles for those who did not bring one.

Gather together. Remind participants that for the first three sessions, they have been exploring the broad sweep of the Old and New Testaments and encountering theories of how, why, and by whom the books contained in them were written. Participants have examined the doctrines of verbal, plenary inspiration and whether or not Scripture is inerrant. Invite the group to make any observations and comments or suggest questions that have arisen out of the discussions in these sessions.

From this point on, the group will be using this background as a foundation for wrestling with some difficult issues in the Bible. Invite someone to read aloud Genesis 32:22-32 (a passage read in the last session). Ask the group to reflect on how Jacob wrestled with God, refusing to let go unless God blessed him. Suggest that when we wrestle with Scripture and open ourselves to the Holy Spirit moving in and through it, we may, like Jacob, discover that we bear in our souls the marks of that encounter, and we can also be assured of God's blessing.

Remind the group that because many activities call for personal sharing, confidentiality is essential. Group members should never pass along stories that have been shared in the group.

Opening Prayer

O God, we come together to wrestle with portions of your story—which is our story, too. We ask for your sustaining presence so that we stay the course, knowing your blessing awaits all those who encounter the Scripture together. Amen.

LEARNING TOGETHER

Video Study and Discussion

Remind the group that as part of their fifteen-minute tour of the Old Testament in Chapter 3, Adam Hamilton asserts that the first eleven chapters of Genesis are primeval and archetypal—their point is to tell us about ourselves and about God. That understanding helps inform how we wrestle with the questions in today's session.

Invite the group to listen in the video for how Hamilton defines the truth of these early stories. Also suggest that group members jot down the dates Hamilton gives for milestones in the origin of the earth and its inhabitants.

After viewing the video, discuss:

- What are the truths Hamilton suggests these early stories in Genesis are communicating?

- Do you consider these truths to be in conflict with scientific truths about the earth's origin?

If so, why? If not, how would you characterize
the relationship between these truths and science?

Invite the group to make a timeline of the prevailing
scientific consensus about the creation of the earth. Tape
a large sheet of paper to the wall horizontally, and add
dates to a horizontal line as the group names them from
their notes. (They can also refer to Chapter 19 in the
text.)

Now invite the group to view the YouTube video
of *God's Trombones*, described earlier in this chapter
under Special Preparation. Afterward, invite the group to
reflect silently on the differences in the timeline based on
scientific consensus and the video that presents a contemporary poetic rendition of the Creation story in Genesis 1.
The group will delve further into an analysis of that
comparison shortly.

Book Study and Discussion

Adam Hamilton observes in Chapter 19 that a lit-
eralist or creationist reading of the Bible sets up a false
dichotomy in which one must choose between science
and the Bible. To further explore what he means, do a
comparison of the creation accounts in Genesis 1 and 2.

Distribute paper and pens or pencils. Form pairs and
invite one person in each pair to examine Genesis 1 and
the other Genesis 2:4-10. Encourage the pairs to read
both the assigned Scripture and the relevant material

in book Chapter 19. First ask each person to chart the account of creation found in his or her passage. Then have the partners compare their accounts.

Ask the pairs to discuss the two accounts and answer the following:

- Does either account sound like a science lesson? Why or why not?

- Hamilton observes that Genesis 1 is a creed. What would you say is the purpose or lesson of the second account?

Invite volunteers to read aloud Genesis 3. Discuss:

- Hamilton says this biblical story is our story. In what way would you say that is true?

- As you reflect on what has been said in your group session about the biblical account and the scientific explanations about creation, what observations can you make about the nature, reliability, and credibility of truth?

Adam and Eve

In considering the question of whether Adam and Eve were real people, revisit the timeline and add the dates Hamilton cites when discussing Adam and Eve in Chapter 19, when *homo sapiens* began creating musical instruments, when they started creating more complex artwork, and the like.

Hamilton tells us that the names Adam and Eve, found in the story of the Fall in Genesis 3 but not in the second account of creation, are representational. That is, in Hebrew *Adam* simply means man and *Eve* means life or bearer of life. Show the group *The Creation of Adam* by Michelangelo, one of the images in the fresco of the Sistine Chapel ceiling. Invite them to imagine that this painting could depict the moment when God breathed the breath of life.

- Hamilton posits that Adam and Eve represent a tipping point in human development when *homo sapiens* began to think at a higher level and started reasoning, creating, and loving, possibly tied to the advent of complex language. How does this hypothesis strike you?

- Along with the ability to reason came the ability to distinguish between right and wrong, as well as the ability to choose. How might this ability be related to "the Fall"?

Dinosaurs on the Ark?

Invite the group to look again at the beginning of book Chapter 2 to locate when scientists believe dinosaurs lived and when the human race came on the scene. Hamilton observes that, as someone who accepts the scientific consensus about the age of the earth, for him the answer to whether there were dinosaurs on the ark is simple: no.

Post the questions you wrote on a large sheet of paper (see Special Preparation earlier in this chapter) in which Hamilton suggests how this story should be read.

Ask a volunteer to read aloud the story of Noah as found in Genesis 6:5-6 and 7:11-23. Then discuss the posted questions. After the discussion, sum up by asking:

- What conclusions can we draw about the story of Noah?

- Why does Hamilton answer the question of whether this account is true by stating, "Sort of"?

Hamilton observes that increased complexity in language may have been associated with more complex and sophisticated weaponry. He suggests that this weaponry may account for the extinction of the Neanderthals. Invite the group to read silently President Eisenhower's words that are quoted toward the end of Chapter 21, which call for limiting the Cold War. Hamilton writes that, as he reads Genesis 6, he can't help but note that since humanity has reached the apex of technological development, the cost in human life to war and violence has been enormous. Invite the group to respond to Eisenhower's words. Do they ring true? What difference has the ending of the Cold War made?

Ask someone to read aloud today's biblical foundation verse, 1 Corinthians 10:11, and have participants respond to the following statements by Adam Hamilton:

Paul's words substantiate the idea that the point of Noah's story was not to teach history, or geology, but to teach us about God and God's will for our lives.

The stories in the first eleven chapters of Genesis … are told less to inform us of ancient history than to teach us about the human condition and about God who created us. As we read them, we are meant to worry less about whether they really happened in exactly the way they are described, and more about the truths God intends us to see in them.

WRAPPING UP

Closing Activity

Distribute art and writing materials to the group. Keeping in mind Hamilton's words about the stories in Genesis and how they are meant to be understood, ask participants to use the materials to create something— a poem, a montage, or another artistic response that expresses their understandings of one or more truths from these stories. For some participants, it might be a response to the biblical accounts, for others, an expression of awe in the face of what science has revealed. In some instances, it might even be a synthesis of the two. After allowing some time for participants to work, display completed expressions around your space. Invite group members to move around, viewing the work in silence.

Review with the group the questions addressed in today's session. Invite them to respond to the following:

- In exploring these stories from Genesis,
  I was struck by …
  I still have some confusion or questions about …
  I want to think further about …

Encourage those who have not yet read the chapters covered today to do so.

Invite the group to read the Genesis stories during their devotional time this week, asking the Holy Spirit to speak in and through the passages. Group members might want to choose a phrase to pray this week, such as "And God saw that it was good" (1:12b) or God's promise: "As long as the earth endures, seedtime and harvest, cold and heat, summer and winter, day and night, shall not cease" (8:22).

Tell the group that in the next session they will explore two troubling questions: why God is portrayed as being violent in some Bible passages, and why there is suffering in the world. In addition, they will consider some questions about the reliability of the Gospel accounts and the veracity of some words attributed to Jesus. Encourage the group to read book Chapters 22–26 in preparation for the session.

Closing Prayer

Creator God, we are in awe of this earth and intrigued by how it might have come into being. Even as we have explored the truths revealed by science, we give thanks for the truths given to us in Scripture about ourselves and about the abundant life you intend for us and all creation. Give us new insights and stir us in new directions. In the name of Jesus Christ. Amen.

5. Violence, Suffering, and Other Troubling Issues

Book Chapters 22–26

Planning the Session

Session Goals

As a result of conversations and activities connected with this session, group members should begin to:

- explore the seeming contradiction between the God of love revealed in Jesus Christ and the God who appears sometimes as angry, harsh, and even unjust;

- be introduced to the concept of progressive revelation and examine its implications;

- evaluate two understandings of divine providence—God the micromanager and God the absentee landlord—and formulate a more nuanced understanding of the term;

- explain the difference between undergoing suffering as a punishment and experiencing consequences of one's actions;

- explore the challenges involved in understanding suffering as a punishment or a test;

- choose from among the following for further exploration: the reliability and trustworthiness of the New Testament accounts, the question of how literally to take some of the sayings of Jesus, and the question of whether one must accept Jesus as personal Savior in order to go to heaven.

Biblical Foundation

You will be in the right, O LORD, when I lay charges against you; but let me put my case to you. Why does the way of the guilty prosper? Why do all who are treacherous thrive?

Jeremiah 12:1

Special Preparation

- If you have been doing so, continue to provide iced tea and lemonade.

- **This session and the final session attempt to address some of the questions and issues with which Christians wrestle. As a result, the activities suggested here cover a broad range of issues—probably more than can be handled in a one-hour session. With that in mind, read the suggested session plans and choose the issues you think will work best in your group.**

- On a large sheet of paper, write the following: Joshua and the Battle of Jericho; Jonah and the Big Fish.

- You will need several large sheets of blank paper and markers. Additionally, you'll need either three tables arranged around your space or wall space for posting the paper in three different locations.

- If possible, obtain a recording of Bob Dylan's "With God on Our Side" and a music player.

GETTING STARTED

Opening Activity

Welcome participants as they arrive. Provide Bibles for those who did not bring one.

Gather together as a large group. Call attention to the large sheets of paper displaying the questions group members posed in the first session of the study. Tell them that in this session, you will address the questions of violence and suffering in the Bible as a large group, with additional questions being addressed in smaller groups.

Opening Prayer

Eternal God, we long to know you as we are known. Be present to us as we seek to discern your nature and will. Guide us as we encounter you in Scripture and in the person of your son, the Word made flesh. Amen.

Learning Together

Video Study and Discussion

Set the stage for viewing the video segment by asking participants to respond to the two posted biblical story titles: Joshua and the Battle of Jericho; Jonah and the Big Fish. What do they remember about each of the stories? Ask the group, as they watch the video segment, to think about how these two stories serve to point up some difficult questions about the way God sometimes appears angry, harsh, and even unjust in the Bible.

After viewing the video, invite volunteers to summarize briefly the marked contrasts in the way God is portrayed in the stories of (a) Joshua and how God commanded him to deal with Jericho and (b) what transpired between Jonah and God concerning the Ninevites. Then discuss the questions Adam Hamilton poses:

- Who changed—God or human beings?

- What does Hamilton have to say about "progressive revelation"?

- What are some contemporary examples cited by Hamilton of trying to make God fit cultural norms?

Book Study and Discussion
The Problem of Violence

Adam Hamilton observes that of the 23,000 verses in the Old Testament, only a few hundred portray God acting in violent or unjust ways. Far more often God is portrayed as merciful, slow to anger, and abounding in steadfast love.

Form two small groups to explore two issues in the Old Testament that Hamilton discusses in book Chapter 22: the death penalty and God's anger and wrath. Ask group members to read and discuss the information given in the book regarding these two issues, as well as some of the relevant Scripture passages; then have each group briefly summarize the main points.

In the large group, consider the issue of genocide in the name of God. Ask volunteers to read aloud

Deuteronomy 20:16-18 and Joshua 6:20*b*-21, examples of God's command to completely destroy a people. Invite someone to read aloud the excerpt Hamilton includes from the Moabite stone near the end of book Chapter 22.

Discuss Hamilton's two possible solutions to the moral and theological dilemma of a God who seems to use and to command violence. Discuss:

- Which of the solutions seems most plausibly to explain these texts to you? Why?

- Hamilton observes that the most important reason for reading Joshua is to remind us of how easy it is for people of faith to invoke God's name in the pursuit of violence. What examples can you cite, from history or from our recent past, when someone invoked the name of God and claimed God's blessing for an act of violence or war?

If you were able to obtain a recording of Bob Dylan's "With God on Our Side," play it for the group.

The Problem of Suffering

Ask participants to read over the material at the beginning of book Chapter 23 about divine providence. Designate one side of the classroom space as "God the micromanager" and the other as "God the absentee land-lord." Ask the participants to arrange themselves in the room according to their own views about God's way of superintending what happens here on earth, and then discuss:

- Adam Hamilton notes that for the biblical authors, almost everything they could not explain was attributed to God's providence. What are some examples of these attributions?

Revisit what Hamilton says about the gospel of prosperity. He observes in the book that, although the orthodox position on providence was that the good would prosper and be blessed and the wicked would be punished, there are Bible passages that challenge this position.

Invite volunteers to recount briefly the story of Job as described in Chapter 23. Discuss:

- What two things does Hamilton say are happening in Job?

- Hamilton notes that in some ways Job is a parable set to verse. Do you agree with this description? How might you describe it?

- What challenges are involved in understanding suffering as a punishment and as a test?

- Hamilton suggests that the idea of Christ atoning for our sins may free us from the burden of thinking that our suffering is a punishment. Do you agree? Why or why not?

- What are some differences between viewing suffering as punishment and seeing it as an understanding that actions have consequences?

- What are the pitfalls in the statement "Everything happens for a reason"?

Invite a volunteer to read the quotation from the newspaper clipping cited by Hamilton in Chapter 23, and ask participants to respond. Is the clipping helpful? What would participants add or qualify?

New Testament Musings

Tell the group that the final three chapters for this session deal with issues and questions related to the New Testament: the reliability and trustworthiness of the New Testament accounts, the question of how literally to take some of the sayings of Jesus, and the question of whether one must accept Jesus as personal Savior in order to go to heaven. Ask group members to consider which of these issues is most compelling to them and to arrange themselves in three small groups to consider these three chapters.

Give each small group a large sheet of paper and a marker. Ask the groups to scan their chapter and formulate what they see as the key question addressed in the chapter. (Note: the key question may or may not be named in the chapter title.) Groups should write the question at the top of their sheet, then below it list significant issues addressed in the chapter. Finally, have each group choose a short quotation that expresses a key understanding on their sheet.

Allow time for each small group to work. Then place the large sheets of paper on tables or post them at intervals around the space. Invite participants to visit each of the other groups' sheets and read over the information. On an accompanying blank large sheet of paper, ask participants to jot down observations and print any questions or issues that need clarification.

Back in the large group, ask each small group to present its information briefly. Discuss the additional notations made by members of other groups.

WRAPPING UP

Closing Activity

Review the questions and issues the group has covered in this session. Discuss:

- In Chapter 22, Adam Hamilton observes that if we recognize the Bible's humanity—that it was written by human beings whose understanding and experience of God was shaped by their culture, theological assumptions, and the time in which they lived—then we might be able to say that some biblical texts represented what they believed about God rather than what God actually inspired them to say. How does this understanding help us as we consider difficult passages? What other understandings might help us consider the passages?

- How is our own understanding and experience of God shaped by our culture, theological assumptions, and the time in which we live? Are we being shaped in ways we may not understand, for example, the prevailing civil religion or a zealous patriotism?

- In what ways can the life and ministry of Jesus Christ serve as a corrective measuring stick or lens?

Tell the group that the final session of the study will look at a variety of questions and issues, which may or may not be related. Encourage group members to read book Chapters 27–32 in preparation for the final session. Also invite a volunteer or two to be prepared to make a very brief report on Chapter 30, "Making Sense of the Book of Revelation."

Closing Prayer

Ask participants to reflect on questions and issues with which they continue to struggle. Say that you will open with a word of prayer, then invite them to bring before God the concerns or questions they have. After each is named aloud, the group responds by saying, "*Lord, in your mercy, hear our prayer.*"

Gracious God, we are troubled by many questions and concerns. We wonder why this world is a place where violence seems to prevail. We struggle to reconcile your loving care with the suffering we often experience or observe. We give thanks for this time when we can bring before you our concerns and questions.

[Allow time for concerns and questions to be named.]

We bring all these we have named, and others that we hold in our hearts, before you. Amen.

6. WRESTLING WITH ISSUES OF SEXUALITY AND RELATIONSHIPS

BOOK CHAPTERS 27–32

PLANNING THE SESSION

Session Goals

As a result of conversations and activities connected with this session, group members should begin to:

- explore the view that male dominance was one result of sin and the Fall, and the implications for evaluating the role of women in Scripture;

- wrestle with understandings of homosexuality and the Bible using the process of Mutual Invitation;

- consider into which categories the Scriptures about same-sex relationships might fit and how they might be viewed;

- articulate a clear view of Scripture that recognizes both its divine inspiration and its humanity;

- explore approaches to Bible study and commit to an ongoing dialogue with Scripture in daily life.

Biblical Foundation

So God created humankind in his image,
 in the image of God he created them;
 male and female he created them.

Genesis 1:27

There is no longer Jew or Greek, there is no longer slave or free, there is no longer male and female; for all of you are one in Christ Jesus.

Galatians 3:28

Special Preparation

- If you have been doing so, continue to provide iced tea and lemonade.

- On a large sheet of paper, print the ancient Jewish blessing from Chapter 27: "Blessed are you O God, King of the Universe, Who has not made me a woman."

- On a large sheet of paper, post the following open-ended prompts:
  In learning more aboutthe Bible in this study, I was struck by …
  I still have some confusion or questions about …
  I want to think further about …

- **This final session addresses some of the questions and issues about which Christians are most troubled, particularly those dealing with homosexuality. The suggested process for discussing the issue of homosexuality is Mutual Invitation, an approach developed by Eric H. F. Law. Read over the directions for the activity in advance. If your group is larger than eight or ten, plan to form two or more small groups and recruit participants to facilitate each group. If you need further clarification about the process, do an Internet search for Mutual Invitation. One helpful link is www.kscopeinstitute.org/2007-05 _Kaleidoscope_newsletter_final.pdf.**

- Be prepared to make some suggestions of study materials or devotional guides that may be helpful to participants as they commit to more regular Bible study and reflection in the coming days.

- **Remember that there are more activities than most groups will have time to complete.**

As leader, you'll want to go over the session plan in advance and select the activities you think will work best for your group in the time allotted.

Getting Started

Opening Activity

Welcome participants as they arrive. Provide Bibles for those who did not bring one.

Gather together. Invite the group to revisit the questions they identified in the first session. Review some subsequent questions with which the group has wrestled. Invite participants to make any observations about the previous session or any insights that may have surfaced during the past week.

Invite those who volunteered last session to briefly present a summary of Chapter 30, "Making Sense of the Book of Revelation." Remind the group of the following question from the previous session:

- How is our own understanding and experience of God shaped by our culture, theological assumptions, and the time in which we live? Are we being shaped in ways we may not understand by, for example, the prevailing civil religion or a zealous patriotism?

In Hamilton's comments on Revelation in Chapter 30, he says that John tells us God alone is worthy of our worship and warns us that Rome's interest is power and control and that pledging allegiance to Rome is idolatry. What are the parallels and dangers in our context?

Tell the group that the bulk of the remaining time in this session will focus on homosexuality, one of the most troubling issues to many Christians.

Opening Prayer

Eternal God, we trust in the assurance that wherever two or three are gathered together, there your Spirit will be present. We give thanks for the community of faith, where we can gather with others to wrestle with whatever concerns are laid on our hearts. Guide us today as we conclude this study, and keep us open to fresh understandings and insights that can lead to continued growth. In the name of Jesus Christ. Amen.

LEARNING TOGETHER

Video Study and Discussion

To prepare the group for viewing this video segment, tell them that Adam Hamilton introduces the topic of slavery. Ask them why and how he addresses this issue, and in what ways the issue sheds light on some other topics: the role of women, sex, and homosexuality.

Group members may want to jot down some notes about what Hamilton says concerning these topics, for use later in the discussion.

Following the video, invite someone to summarize the point Hamilton makes about the Bible's position on slavery. Invite others to make any additional points, and jot these down on a large sheet of paper. Tell the group that as they delve more deeply into the role of women, sex, and homosexuality, the principles Hamilton uses in his argument about the Bible and slavery will be important. Note that these are the same basic points Hamilton made in the previous discussion of God and violence as revealed in some Bible passages.

Book Study and Discussion

Remind the group that throughout his book, Hamilton has stated the view that Scripture—especially those Scriptures that are troubling—should be interpreted in light of the fact that Jesus is the Word by which all other words should be understood. Specifically, Bible passages should be interpreted in light of those Scriptures that Jesus said summarized the Law and the Prophets: the Great Commandments and the Golden Rule.

Encourage participants to spend some time reading in book Chapter 31 about the history of religious liberals and conservatives, especially the origin of the term *fundamentalist*. Group members might want to reflect on how many of the five "fundamentals" they themselves adhere to. Also, if they have not already done so, urge them to read book Chapter 28 and to consider honestly if there are Bible passages they choose to take literally while ignoring others. When group members pick and choose in this way, what criteria are they using?

The Role of Women

Ask a man to read aloud the ancient Jewish blessing from Chapter 27 that you have written on a large sheet of paper, and invite the group to respond. Ask:

- If you are a man, how do you respond?

- If you are a woman, how do you respond?

- Do you think this blessing represents the will of God for either sex? Why or why not?

Remind the group that Adam Hamilton has argued throughout his book that it's important in looking at troubling Scriptures to discern which passages reflect the culture and context of their time and which reflect the timeless will of God. Some of the most persuasive passages cited by conservative Christians in advocating an inferior status for women come from the apostle Paul. In order to explore Paul's position further, invite the group to revisit the archetypal stories of Creation and the Fall in Genesis upon which Paul based his position.

Ask half the group to scan Genesis 1:1–2:4a and the other half to scan Genesis 2:4b-24. Discuss:

- What views of gender do you see presented in each account?

- What does Hamilton tell us about the understanding of the word *helper* (*ezer*) in the second creation account?

Ask the group to review silently the story of the Fall in Genesis 3 and respond to the following observation Hamilton makes:

> Whether you take this story literally, or archetypally and figuratively as I do, it is clear that male dominance was a result of sin and the Fall.

Ask the group to name some of the instances from Scripture that Hamilton names that support his then-eight-year-old daughter's assertion: "Daddy, this book is almost all about boys, and when there are girls, they aren't treated very nicely." Ask:

- If you had this conversation with your young daughter and she made a similar observation, how would you respond? How would you respond to a son?

Ask the group to respond to the following from the end of Chapter 27:

In the beginning, God's will was partnership. Sin brought patriarchy. Shouldn't the ideal of redemption be a return to partnership and an end to the subordination of women? And if this is the case, is it not time to recognize that Paul's words about women remaining silent do not reflect God's timeless will for the role women are to play in the church?

Using Mutual Invitation to Discuss Homosexuality

Because homosexuality continues to be one of the most challenging and divisive issues for Christians, it is likely that you will have differing views on the subject in your group. To help bridge this gap and encourage group members to listen to each other, tell the group that they will discuss the issue using a process called Mutual Invitation, which was developed by Eric H. F. Law.

Invite the group to form a circle. If the group is larger than eight or ten, you may want to form two or more smaller circles of chairs. Tell the group that Mutual Invitation is designed to ensure that everyone who wishes to speak has an equal opportunity to do so. Encourage the group to commit to listening to each other with the respect that should characterize the community of faith, whether those in the community agree or not.

The facilitator will begin the discussion of a question by commenting, then he or she will invite someone else in the circle by name to comment. (It need not be the persons sitting on either side of the facilitator.)

That person makes his or her comments and invites someone else. The process continues until everyone has had a chance to respond. If a person is not ready yet to speak, he or she can say "Pass for now" and invite someone else, in which case the facilitator makes sure that the skipped person has another chance to speak. A participant may also say "Pass," indicating that the person does not want to comment on the question at all. You may want to set a time limit for individual comments, perhaps no more than one or two minutes each. The idea is to give every individual an opportunity to comment without the need for group discussion. The group can decide whether each member will speak just once or more than once. If more than once, it is important that everyone must have an opportunity to speak before anyone can speak a second time.

Before beginning the process, ask volunteers to read aloud the following passages: Genesis 19:1-11; Leviticus 18:22 and 20:13; Romans 1:18-27. Then invite the group to use Mutual Invitation to respond to one or more of Adam Hamilton's questions and comments:

- Is this story (Genesis 19:1-11) about men entering into loving, committed same-sex relationships with one other, or is this story about the attempted gang-rape of two strangers by the men of the town? If the town's men had gang-raped Lot's daughters, would it have constituted an indictment against heterosexual

sexual intimacy? Do you think the men of Sodom considered themselves homosexuals? Or was their attack on strangers a way of demonstrating power over the strangers and perhaps humiliating them?

• What was it that Moses had in mind when he prescribed the death penalty in the Leviticus passages? Discuss the ideas Hamilton presents in Chapter 29 about the passages.

• What does Paul have in mind when he takes up the issue in Romans?

• Is it possible that this handful of verses that condemn same-sex relationships may be similar to other verses, such as those affirming slavery, that seem out of sync with God's will as we understand it today?

After allowing time for the group to engage in Mutual Invitation, call attention to Hamilton's observation that biblical passages can be placed in three broad categories or "buckets." These categories are passages that (1) reflect the timeless will of God for human beings, (2) reflect God's will in a particular time but not for all time, and (3) reflect the culture and historical circumstances in which they were written but never reflected God's will.

Ask the group to reflect in silence on the following:

- To which of the three categories do I believe the passages about same-sex relationships belong?

- What kinds of interactions have I had with gay and lesbian persons, and how have these interactions influenced my understanding of this issue?

Ask someone to read aloud the final two paragraphs of Chapter 29. Encourage group members to keep the dialogue open now and in the future, even as they are realistic about the strong feelings and opinions on this issue held by persons within the group and in the larger community of faith.

How to Read the Bible

As a way of discussing the postscript, "Reading the Bible for All It's Worth," form eight small groups and assign each small group one of Hamilton's eight numbered suggestions for reading the Bible. Ask the members of each small group to read over the material in the text about how to read the Bible using that particular numbered approach. After allowing a few minutes, invite each small group to report their thoughts and findings to the large group. If participants have already used a particular approach and found it useful, ask them to comment; or if they have used a variation, invite their observations on how that worked.

Wrapping Up

Closing Activity

Call attention to the questions the group formulated in Session 1. Point out that some, but certainly not all, of their questions may have been answered, nor have all the troubling issues been resolved. And that is as it should be! When we wrestle with Scripture, individually and in groups, the Holy Spirit is present with us. That Spirit comforts and sustains, but it also stirs up and unsettles and makes us restless to know God more fully.

Ask a volunteer to read aloud the final paragraph of Hamilton's book. Then distribute index cards or postcards, along with pens or pencils. Ask participants to reflect in silence on a commitment they might make as a result of this study to read the Bible more intentionally and with more regularity. If you have suggestions of study materials or devotional guides, offer those to the group. Then ask them to jot down on one side of the card a commitment they will make— something as simple as setting aside ten minutes a day to read the Bible, or a more ambitious goal. On the other side, have them print their name and address if you are using postcards, or their e-mail address if using index cards. Tell them that you will mail or e-mail a reminder in a month's time.

Closing Prayer

Form a circle, join hands and close with a time of prayer:

Loving God, we give thanks for this time together. Together, we have wrestled with your Scriptures, confident in the knowledge that where two or three are gathered together, there your Spirit will be present. Hear us now as we offer our prayers up to you. [Invite the person to your left to pray a sentence prayer, then the next person, and so on until everyone has had an opportunity. If someone chooses not to pray aloud, he or she can simply squeeze the hand of the next person. Conclude by saying:] *And all God's people say, "Amen."*